There Is Never

Anything

but the Present

✄

There Is Never Anything but the Present

but the Present

AND OTHER INSPIRING WORDS

OF WISDOM

Alan Watts

 PANTHEON BOOKS   NEW YORK

Owing to limitations of space, permissions information can be found
on pages 117–120.

LIBRARY OF CONGRESS CATALOGING-IN-PUBLICATION DATA
Name: Watts, Alan, 1915-1973, author.
Title: There is never anything but the present : and other inspiring
words of wisdom / Alan Watts.
Description: First edition. Pantheon Books, New York :
Pantheon Books, 2021.
Identifiers: LCCN 2021015936 (print). LCCN 2021015937 (ebook).
ISBN 9780593316023 (hardcover). ISBN 9780593316030 (ebook).
Subjects: LCSH: Wisdom-Quotations, maxims, etc. Conduct of life-
Quotations, maxims, etc. Life-Quotations, maxims, etc.
Classification: LCC BJ1595 .W335 2021 (print) |
LCC BJ1595 (ebook) | DDC 158-dc23
LC record available at lccn.loc.gov/2021015936
LC ebook record available at lccn.loc.gov/2021015937

www.pantheonbooks.com

Jacket design by Gray318

Printed in Canada
First Edition

2 4 6 8 9 7 5 3 1

There Is Never Anything but the Present

Never pretend to a love which you do not
actually feel, for love is not ours to command.

When no risk is taken there is no freedom.

The only way to make sense out of change is to plunge into it, move with it, and join the dance.

No one imagines that a symphony is supposed to improve in quality as it goes along, or that the whole object of playing it is to reach the finale. The point of music is discovered in every moment of playing and listening to it. It is the same, I feel, with the greater part of our lives, and if we are unduly absorbed in improving them we may forget altogether to live them.

The individual is an aperture through which the whole energy of the universe is aware of itself.

What we have forgotten is that thoughts and words are *conventions*, and that it is fatal to take conventions too seriously. A convention is a social convenience, as, for example, money . . . But it is absurd to take money too seriously, to confuse it with real wealth.

We do not "come into" this world; we come *out* of it, as leaves from a tree. As the ocean "waves," the universe "peoples." Every individual is an expression of the whole realm of nature, a unique action of the total universe.

To see the light, it is only necessary to stop
dreaming and open the eyes.

The human organism has the same kind of innate intelligence as the ecosystems of nature, and the wisdom of the nerves and senses must be watched with patience and respect.

❧

If a problem can be solved at all, to understand
it and to know what to do about it are
the same thing.

So long as one thinks about listening,
one cannot hear clearly, and so long as one thinks
about trying or not trying to let go of oneself,
one cannot let go. Yet whether one thinks about
listening or not, the ears are hearing just the
same, and nothing can stop the sound from
reaching them.

If you don't have anything to say, not even
the greatest mastery of English will long stand
you in good stead.

Faith is not clinging but letting go.

To be afraid of life is to be afraid of yourself.

Problems that remain persistently insoluble
should always be suspected as questions
asked in the wrong way.

❦

Neither an individual nor a society can pull itself up by its own bootstraps, even though it is now commonly being said that this is precisely what we must do. So long as we use force, whether physical or moral, to improve the world and ourselves, we are squandering energy that might otherwise be used for things which *can* be done.

∞

What is true and positive is too real
and too living to be described, and to try
to describe it is like putting red paint
on a red rose.

Muddy water is best cleared
by leaving it alone.

Trust in human nature is acceptance of the
good-and-bad of it, and it is hard to trust those
who do not admit their own weaknesses.

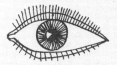

Because the idea is so much more
comprehensible than the reality, the symbol
so much more stable than the fact, we learn
to identify ourselves with our idea
of ourselves.

To feel that life is meaningless unless "I" can be permanent is like having fallen desperately in love with an inch.

The desire for security and the feeling of insecurity are the same thing. To hold your breath is to lose your breath.

We do not dance to reach a certain point
on the floor, but simply to dance.

It is not so much a matter of what you do as of how you do it, not so much the content as the style of action adopted.

Paradoxical as it may seem, the purposeful life has no content, no point. It hurries on and on, and misses everything. Not hurrying, the purposeless life misses nothing, for it is only when there is no goal and no rush that the human senses are fully open to receive the world.

☙

The anxiety-laden problem of what will happen to me when I die is, after all, like asking what happens to my fist when I open my hand, or where my lap goes when I stand up.

We suffer from the delusion that the entire universe is held in order by the categories of human thought, fearing that if we do not hold to them with the utmost tenacity, everything will vanish into chaos.

Transitoriness is depressing only to the mind
which insists upon trying to grasp.

Life thrusts us into the unknown willy-nilly,
and resistance is as futile and exasperating as
trying to swim against a roaring torrent.

There is a point where thinking—like boiling an egg—must come to a stop.

· The greatest hinderance to objective knowledge
is our own subjective presence.

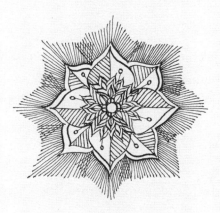

If the universe is meaningless, so is the statement that it is so. If this world is a vicious trap, so is its accuser, and the pot is calling the kettle black.

Real religion is the transformation
of anxiety into laughter.

The greater part of human activity is designed to make permanent those experiences and joys which are only lovable because they are changing. Music is a delight because of its rhythm and flow. Yet the moment you arrest the flow and prolong a note or chord beyond its time, the rhythm is destroyed.

Great power is worry, and total power is
boredom, such that even God renounces it and
pretends, instead, that he is people and fish
and insects and plants.

The mind *must* be interested or absorbed in something, just as a mirror must always be reflecting something. When it is not trying to be interested in itself—as if a mirror would reflect itself—it must be interested, or absorbed, in other people and things.

When you no longer make the distinction
between the universe and how you are acting
upon it, you are really on your own and so
acquire a sense of responsibility.

Egoism is like trying to swim without relying on the water, endeavoring to keep afloat by tugging at your own legs; your whole body becomes tense, and you sink like a stone.

I have had the privilege, especially in recent years, of seeing what I believe to be very deeply into the heart of this universe and its life—and there isn't anything to be afraid of. The end and bottom of it all is not emptiness, but a love beyond anyone's imagination.

We have never . . . permitted ourselves to be
everything that we are, to see that fundamentally
all the gains and losses, rights and wrongs of our
lives are as natural and "perfect" as the peaks
and valleys of a mountain range.

As we now know him, the human being seems
to be a trap set to catch himself.

Trying to please the brain is like trying to drink through your ears.

Man is not to be an intellectual porcupine,
meeting his environment with a surface
of spikes.

∞

Hurrying and delaying are alike ways of trying
to resist the present.

Good without evil is like up without down.

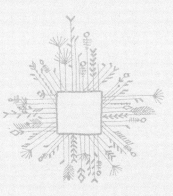

To understand music, you must listen to it.
But so long as you are thinking, "*I* am listening
to this music," you are not listening.

I simply feel that a human being must always recognize that he is qualitatively more than any system of thought he can imagine, and therefore he should never label himself. He degrades himself when he does.

The spiritual is not to be separated from
the material, nor the wonderful
from the ordinary.

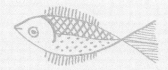

A chest of gold coins or a fat wallet of bills is of no use whatsoever to a wrecked sailor alone on a raft.

There will be respect for authority when, and only when, authority is itself respectable.

[Zen] enters into everything wholeheartedly and freely without having to keep an eye on itself. It does not confuse spirituality with thinking about God while one is peeling potatoes. Zen spirituality is just to peel the potatoes.

The words which one might be tempted
to use for a silent and wide-open mind are
mostly terms of abuse—thoughtless, mindless,
unthinking, empty-headed, and vague. Perhaps
this is some measure of an innate fear of
releasing the chronic cramp of consciousness
by which we grasp the facts of life and
manage the world.

❧

The more one studies attempted solutions to problems in politics and economics, in art, philosophy, and religion, the more one has the impression of extremely gifted people wearing out their ingenuity at the impossible and futile task of trying to get the water of life into neat and permanent packages.

✢

One has only to consider how cold and desolate the fairest face of nature can seem to a man left utterly alone, willing to exchange the whole sum of natural beauty for a single human face.

We keep reactivating the past in the hope that history is guiding us to where we should be going in the future, and this is driving the car with eyes glued to the rear-vision mirror.

❧

Running away from fear is fear, fighting pain is pain, trying to be brave is being scared. If the mind is in pain, the mind is pain. The thinker has no other form than his thought. There is no escape. But so long as you are not aware of the inseparability of thinker and thought, you will try to escape.

∞

If happiness always depends on something
expected in the future, we are chasing a
will-o'-the-wisp that ever eludes our grasp,
until the future, and ourselves, vanish.

To succeed is always to fail—in the sense that the more one succeeds in anything, the greater is the need to go on succeeding. To eat is to survive to be hungry.

Instead of thinking "I walk," you think, "There is a walking," until you begin to see yourself as a part of the Universe not separate from other parts while the "I" is as the whole.

Nirvana can only arise unintentionally, spontaneously, when the impossibility of self-grasping has been thoroughly perceived.

You cannot understand life and its mysteries
as long as you try to grasp it. Indeed, you cannot
grasp it, just as you cannot walk off with a river
in a bucket. If you try to capture running water
in a bucket, it is clear that you do not understand
it and that you will always be disappointed,
for in the bucket the water does not run.

No one is more dangerously insane than one
who is sane all the time: he is like a steel bridge
without flexibility, and the order of his life
is rigid and brittle.

Love is the organizing and unifying principle which makes the world a *universe* . . . It is the very essence and character of mind, and becomes manifest in action when the mind is whole.

Spiritual awakening is the difficult process
whereby the increasing realization that
everything is as wrong as it can be flips suddenly
into the realization that everything is as right
as it can be. Or better, everything is as It
as it can be.

Tomorrow and plans for tomorrow can have no significance at all unless you are in full contact with the reality of the present, since it is in the present and *only* in the present that you live.

To get rid of what is passed on to you, you have to develop a forgettory instead of a memory.

You didn't come into this world. You came out
of it, like a wave from the ocean. You are not
a stranger here.

A living body is not a fixed *thing* but a flowing *event*, like a flame or a whirlpool.

Reason cannot be trusted if the brain
cannot be trusted.

To be forever looking beyond is to remain blind
to what is here.

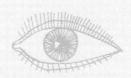

Instant coffee . . . is a well-deserved punishment
for being in a hurry to reach the future.

❧

The perishability and changefulness
of the world is part and parcel of
its liveliness and loveliness.

Knowing what is not so is often quite as important as knowing what is.

Death is the unknown in which all of us lived
before birth.

[A] life full of goals or end-points is like trying to abate one's hunger by eating merely the two precise ends of a banana.

&

There is no problem of how to love. We love.
We are love, and the only problem is the
direction of love, whether it is to go straight out
like sunlight, or to try to turn back on itself.

We feel that our actions are voluntary when they follow a decision, and involuntary when they happen without decision. But if decision itself were voluntary, every decision would have to be preceded by a decision to decide—an infinite regression which fortunately does not occur.

When we have made up our minds as to what
we *do* want, there remain indeed many practical
and technical problems. But there is no point
at all in discussing these until we have made
up our minds.

I cannot throw a ball so long as I am holding on to it—so as to maintain perfect control of its movement.

Much of the secret of life consists in knowing how to laugh, and also how to breathe.

Unless one is able to live fully in the present, the future is a hoax. There is no point whatever in making plans for a future which you will never be able to enjoy. When your plans mature, you will still be living for some other future beyond.

∞

To stand face to face with insecurity is still not to understand it. To understand it, you must not face it but be it.

A man rings like a cracked bell when he thinks
and acts with a split mind—one part standing
aside to interfere with the other, to control,
to condemn, or to admire.

One of the highest pleasures is to be more or less unconscious of one's own existence, to be absorbed in interesting sights, sounds, places, and people. Conversely, one of the greatest pains is to be self-conscious, to feel unabsorbed and cut off from the community and the surrounding world.

Childlikeness, or artless simplicity, is the ideal
of the artist no less than of the sage, for it is
to perform the work of art or of life without
the least trace of affectation, of being in
two minds.

Just as true humor is laughter at oneself, true humanity is knowledge of oneself.

Like too much alcohol, self-consciousness makes us see ourselves double, and we make the double image for two selves—mental and material, controlling and controlled, reflective and spontaneous. Thus instead of suffering we suffer about suffering, and suffer about suffering about suffering.

ॐ

There is no other reality than present reality,
so that, even if one were to live for endless ages,
to live for the future would be to miss the
point everlastingly.

∞

To be silent is not to lose your tongue. On the contrary, it is only through silence that one can discover something new to talk about.

Not content with tasting the food, I am also trying to taste my tongue. Not content with feeling happy, I want to feel myself feeling happy—so as to be sure not to miss anything.

The answer to the problem of suffering is not away from the problem but in it. The inevitability of pain will not be met by deadening sensitivity but by increasing it, by exploring and feeling out the manner in which the natural organism itself wants to react and which its innate wisdom has provided.

I could make a strong, if not conclusive, case for the idea that plants are more intelligent than people—more beautiful, more pacific, more ingenious in their ways of reproduction, more at home in their surroundings, and even more sensitive. Why, we even use flower-forms as our symbols of the divine when the human face reminds us too much of ourselves—the Hindu-Buddhist mandala, the golden lotus, and the Mystic Rose in Dante's vision of Paradise. Nothing else reminds us so much of a star with a living heart.

There is only this *now*. It does not come from anywhere; it is not going anywhere. It is not permanent, but it is not impermanent. Though moving, it is always still. When we try to catch it, it seems to run away, and yet it is always here and there is no escape from it. And when we turn round to find the self which knows this moment, we find that it has vanished like the past.

This—the immediate, everyday, and present experience—is IT, the entire and ultimate point for the existence of a universe.

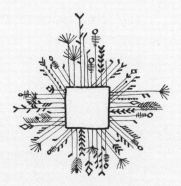

To act or grow creatively we must begin from where we are, but we cannot begin at all if we are not "all here" without reservation or regret. Lacking self-acceptance, we are always at odds with our point of departure, always doubting the ground on which we stand, always so divided against ourselves that we cannot act with sincerity.

You do not play a sonata *in order* to reach the final chord, and if the meanings of things were simply in ends, composers would write nothing but finales.

The more a person knows of himself, the more he will hesitate to define his nature and to assert what he must necessarily feel, and the more he will be astounded at his capacity to feel in unsuspected and unpredictable ways.

Other people teach us who we are. Their attitudes to us are the mirror in which we learn to see ourselves, but the mirror is distorted.

Human desire tends to be insatiable. We are so anxious for pleasure that we can never get enough of it.

∞

Nothing worthwhile is ever achieved
without danger.

I have no other self than the totality of things
of which I am aware.

We get such a kick out of looking forward to
pleasures and rushing ahead to meet them that
we can't slow down enough to enjoy them
when they come.

If you cannot trust yourself, you cannot even trust your mistrust of yourself—so that without this underlying trust in the whole system of nature you are simply paralyzed.

It does not seem to occur to us that
action goaded by a sense of inadequacy
will be creative only in a limited sense.
It will express the emptiness from which
it springs rather than fullness,
hunger rather than strength.

A world in which there are no mysteries
is a familiarity breeding contempt.

Trying to define yourself is like trying to bite your own teeth.

When a man no longer confuses himself with
the definition of himself that others have given
him, he is at once universal and unique.

A world which increasingly consists of destinations without journeys between them, a world which values only "getting somewhere" as fast as possible, becomes a world without substance. One can get anywhere and everywhere, and yet the more this is possible, the less is anywhere and everywhere worth getting to.

The sense of not being free comes from trying to do things which are impossible and even meaningless. You are not "free" to draw a square circle, to live without a head, or to stop certain reflex actions. These are not obstacles to freedom; they are the conditions of freedom.

I am not free to draw a circle if perchance it should turn out to be a square circle. I am not, thank heaven, free to walk out of doors and leave my head at home. Likewise I am not free to live in any moment but this one, or to separate myself from my feelings.

There is never anything but the present,
and if one cannot live there, one cannot
live anywhere.

No amount of working with the muscles of the mouth and tongue will enable us to taste our food more acutely. The eyes and the tongue must be trusted to do the work by themselves.

We seldom realize . . . that our most private thoughts and emotions are not actually our own. For we think in terms of languages and images which we did not invent, but which were given to us by our society.

Normally, we do not so much look at things
as overlook them.

Haven't we
been here
before?

The philosopher Alan Watts (1915-1973) is best known for popularizing Zen Buddhism in the United States and Europe. During his lifetime he wrote more than twenty-five books, including the bestsellers *The Way of Zen* and *The Wisdom of Insecurity*. Born in England, Watts immigrated to the United States in his twenties. His colorful and controversial life, from his school days in England, to his priesthood in the Anglican Church as chaplain of Northwestern University, to his experimentation with psychedelic drugs, made him an icon of the 1960s counterculture movement. Millions of followers continue to be enlightened by his teachings through his books, which have been published in twenty-six countries, and his lectures, which are found worldwide on the internet.

A NOTE ON THE TYPE

The text type in this book was set in Jenson, a font designed for the Adobe Corporation by Robert Slimbach in 1995. Jenson is an interpretation of the famous Venetian type cut in 1469 by the Frenchman Nicolas Jenson (c. 1420–1480).

Composed by North Market Street Graphics
Lancaster, Pennsylvania

Printed and bound by Friesens
Altona, Manitoba

Book design by Pei Loi Koay